MYRIAD

A Collection of Poems

AISHWARYA SETH

notionpress.com

INDIA • SINGAPORE • MALAYSIA

ISBN

Hardcase 979-8-89961-885-7
Paperback 979-8-89724-594-9

Table of Contents

Acknowledgements

Truly, this book exists because of my support village – the people in my corner who have encouraged and supported me, and have had full faith in my abilities.

Thank you for listening to my stories (and wandering through my thoughts, musings, theories, questionable life decisions, and side quests with me). Your support – whether through a kind word, a nudge to keep going, or simply showing up – has meant everything.

And to you, dear reader – whether my words make you feel something, pause for a moment, or just nod along, I truly appreciate you. Thanks for joining me on this adventure. I'm so glad you're here. ❧

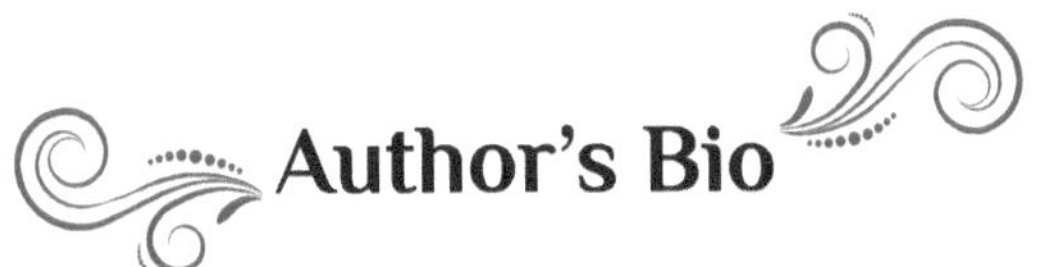

Author's Bio

Aishwarya Seth is first and foremost a storyteller. This whimsical, weird, wonderful woman has many interests and skills – and poetry is one of her finest.

An avid traveller, photographer, and adventurer, she tries to capture her experiences vividly. Her poems often reflect her thoughtful, candid approach to life, evoking empathy and emotions with their relatable imagery.

A voracious reader, Aishwarya grew up in the world of fiction and fantasy and returns there when she can. She honed her storytelling skills as a playwright in her undergraduate years and now uses data science to uncover scientifically and statistically sound stories in human genetics research.

After decades of scribbling her thoughts dramatically in rhyme, Aishwarya has finally found the courage to share this piece of her soul with the world and sincerely hopes that you enjoy the journey this book presents.

PROLOGUE

A Reminder

To be real,
You have to feel.
You have to feel all of it.
The pain, the despair, the sorrow,
The hope and strength drawn from
Gentle promises of tomorrow

FRAGMENTS OF FIRE

Summoned

I watched you walk across the room,
Watched you pace across my shallow tomb
I saw the shadows creep across the floor.
Collapsing: blood marked where you stood before

I heard the sound of shattering glass,
Sensed the adjacent souls gathering,
Memories racing, hearts beating fast

Whatever else had come to pass
It was established now that only ruins last.
The end seemed fitting, you see,
It's fitting that you ended close to me.

It would be the greatest story ever told:
Lingering ghosts with hearts, ice-cold –
Had ended the story in the same way that it began
With broken promises, betrayal,
And one that always abandoned and ran.

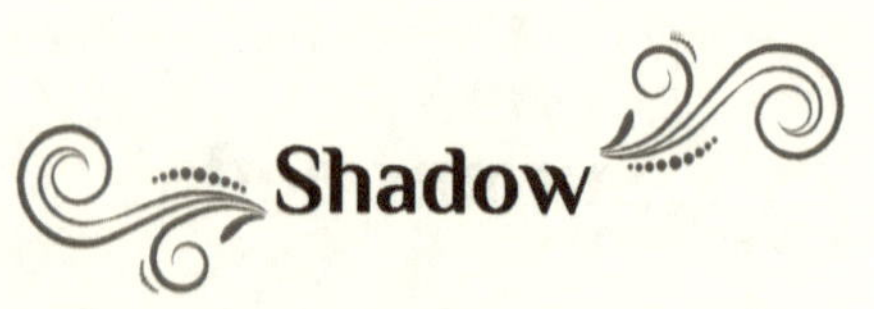

Shadow

There's a shadow lurking in the night.
There's a shadow: just out of sight –
It watches, and breathes, and burns.
It stumbles, it forms, it churns,
Fiercely billowing into raging flames,
It grows and learns but never tames

It watches every step you take,
Haunts every choice you make.
It clings to you.
It knows what you know.
It watches.
It watches the entire show.

It follows,
Patiently waiting for its turn.
It watches,
Patiently waiting until you learn,
To give into it,
And turn to ash and sand once more.
Or to fight it,
And rise stronger than you were before.

It's a part of you,
A lone, watchful ranger.
It's a source of comfort,
A mysterious stranger,
Faithful, like a friend,
Yet an elusive danger.

It's your own little monster,
Your hand-carved cage,
Your buried resentment
Your in-built rage.

With every step you take towards the door,
It follows you – just a little more.
And upward, as the time together trends,
It's harder to decide where you begin and it ends.

It's difficult – that constant struggle:
Shadowed thoughts all in a muddle.
Moments drenched in darkness; no glimmer in sight,
Others in the spotlight,
Shining endlessly bright.

When all seems right but all feels wrong,
You wait through the darkest night for dawn,
As it grows, so do you,
Stronger with each step, seeing it through.

The Warning

The curling flames,
The scorched leaves,
The stormy winds
That replaced the summer breeze.
The torn towers,
The empty halls,
The rotting faces,
And all the kingdom's abandoned places
Are silent observers
Of death & destruction,
The defeat of all preservers.
Screams & cries resound through the land,
Everyone looks for a helping hand.
Heroes rise, but soon they fall
The power of one
Is not as strong as that of all
Behold now! In the darkest hour,
Hope is awoken:
For in an old, forgotten, endless cavern,
The eye of the dragon is open.

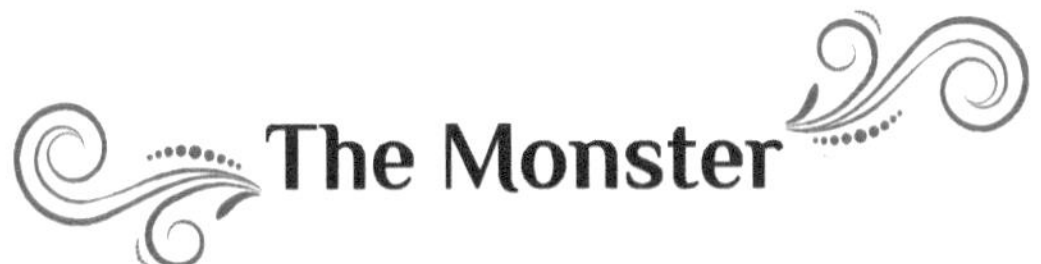

The Monster

The tear-filled eyes
Watch every moment with bated breath
The blood-streaked face
Let's drops of rubies fall; staining the carpet red
The misshapen nose,
The broken teeth
And dilated pupils from an overdose
The bruises bloom everywhere
Screams are there, the walls are bare,
Everything is red
The nail-like claws,
The pounding paws,
And the creaks beneath the bed
You want to stare at everything, but don't you dare
Look away from this vision.
As you watch with anticipation
You see its struggle, you see it strive,
Suddenly, things around seem to fade
Creatures under your bed could not escape
The look of horror on your face
For or against the beliefs of every religion and race
The monster in the mirror smirked and stepped out.
Alive.

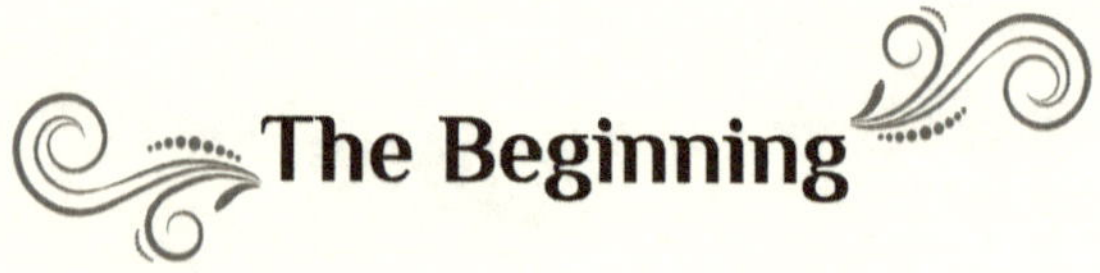 The Beginning

Watch closely, Little One,
The game has just begun.

It begins with a roll of the dice of fate:
Unpredictable as always,
It punishes those who are early or late.

The days of joy are bright and plenty,
Summer's bounty and the Horn of Plenty
The echoes of laughter fill the air,
With smiles of contentment everywhere

Beware
A shadow begins to rise.
And as its power grows,
All that you hold near and dear,
Will disappear before your eyes.
Darkness, torment, and pain accompany every step.
And soon, you'll be screaming out for help.
But you're on your own, you're alone
There is nothing you can do.
Except wait for the eye of the storm to come to you.

Out of the blue,
Hope arises anew,
As the hero's war cry resounds,
The happiness of the people knows no bounds.
They march to battle at full strength;
Fighting until their enemy is spent.
Light descends once more,
And though peace seems to make amends,
Evil lurks nearby, festering,
Waiting for revenge.

When belief fades and doubt creeps in again,
Evil sets up his stronghold,
Gloomy, damp, dark and cold:
Watching his prey creep into his den.

Watch closely, Little One,
For the game of Death has just begun.

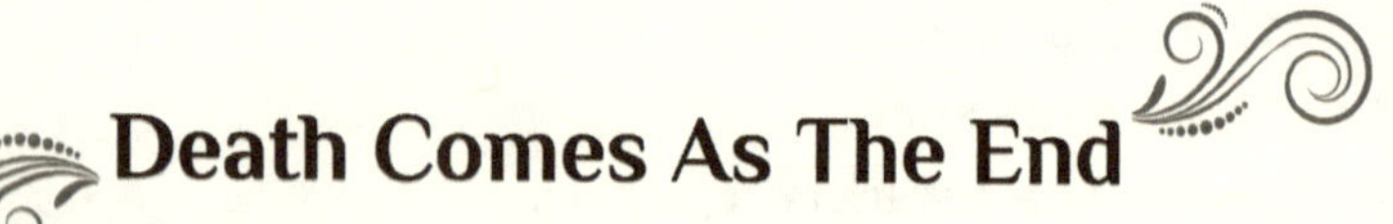 Death Comes As The End

In the peace and quiet of the twilight hour,
The enemy approaches from afar,
Where she lay with her golden head
Fast asleep in her warm bed.

He falters now – a nervous wreck,
Stepping forward, without a sound,
He plunges his knife into her neck
His knife meets flesh; she won't rebound.

For in our lives, there are
Unforeseen events around every bend.
Yet for one and all,
Big and small,
Death comes as the end.

A man walks down the crowded street,
Unaware of the fate he's about to meet.
The sniper hides behind a cart,
His rifle steadily aimed at the heart.
The trigger is pulled – a flash, a roar,
And the man is no more.

For in our lives, there are
Unforeseen events around every bend.
Yet for one and all,
Big and small,
Death comes as the end.

His nephew approaches from behind.
A devilish thought in his mind
A ruthless shove, no sign of grief,
The nephew smirked;
The old man breathed his last in disbelief.

For in our lives, there are
Unforeseen events around every bend.
Yet for one and all,
Big and small,
Death comes as the end.

The enchanting lady sipped her wine,
Graceful, glowing, looking fine,
Suddenly, her face was contorted with pain.
Fire coursing as she fought in vain,
Silent and swift, the poison crept,
Her fading breath: a secret kept.

For in our lives, there are
Unforeseen events around every bend.
Yet for one and all,
Big and small,
Death comes as the end.

The murderer was tormented,
Tortured by the weight of his deeds.
As he walked towards the rope,
It seemed he had forgotten how to breathe.
He hanged himself – that fateful day,
His crimes left many worlds in disarray,
And under the dark sky, gloomy, grey,
His contentious life slipped away...

For in our lives, there are
Unforeseen events around every bend.
Yet for one and all,
Big and small,
Death comes as the end.

A Warrior of Rome

The walls get thinner,
　The lights grow dimmer,
A sea of restless eyes converge
As the Colosseum's crowd begins to surge.

A cursed path with no recourse,
　Staked in shadows,
　　Bereft of mercy and devoid of remorse,
Yearning for retribution,
　Faith, applause!

The fleeting eyes of a million men,
Focused on the Warriors of Rome,
Hoping for a lingering glance of favour,
In an otherwise lonely, blood-stained home.

The voices get louder,
　The conscience – torn,
Blinded by hunger,
　Bound by rage,
Determined to be worthy of a mention.
On an endless page.

Strength is a gift,
Strength is a curse,
Because even when it's all shattering,
When you can't take another battering,
The other seems worse.

A call to arms, a call for aid,
The voices and people fade,
Humanity is a fleeting myth,
Dying echoes in the pit,
Wounds forgotten, lips split,
All forgiven until a fatal hit.

They say it was a good way to go,
One glorious moment,
Lost in the sands forevermore.

WHISPERS & WARNINGS

Words

Words that flow through mind and pen,
Often make you feel strong again,
For no matter where you are or go,
They will remain constant.
Exactly the same – just so.

For even when the times and winds
Conspire to erase
All that a writer writes and a builder builds,
A mark still remains,
The slightest of impressions,
The trace of a different day

These are the scars that words must leave.
And even as you reap joy or grief
A trace that endures – steadfast and true,
Lingering softly,
On pages old and pages new.

These words must be formed and must remain,
For stories from there and back again,
Life collects its toll along the way,
For the peace we seek in disarray.

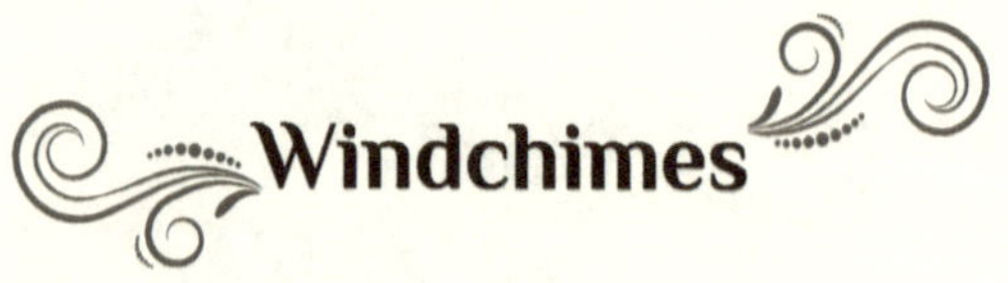

Windchimes

I waited patiently at your door,
Like the countless times I had before,
Waited for your words to reach me,
Me and my ever-yearning ears,
Me – wordlessly brimming with tears,

A grip so desolate and strong,
An unbreakable thread,
Linking us all along,
Familiar but strange all the same,
A melody swirling through my feet,
Remnants of a lifetime on that beat,
The echoes of a long-forgotten song

Moments draw us close, then pull away,
Lost in the woods: abandoned, astray,
The trees offer light, shelter, and shade,
Blurring the lines between:
An endless night, an everlasting day

Meaning drawn from the symbols we speak,
Placeholders that lend warmth to the bleak,
Your words are a mere reflection of my soul,
Fleetingly through and away,
Imperfect in the afterglow.

My feet loop endlessly back,
Until I come full circle,
Headed your way,
Staying long enough for a pause,
No knock, no welcome, no applause.

A broken instrument, forced to chime the only world
it knew,
Forced to retain its story,
Amended, but never anew,
Convoluted, as it repeated, thought, and grew.

Of the story wrought in frame,
Bound for a lifetime,
Drawn from iron,
Embellished in gold.
Forged but once,
Yet endlessly told.

Jaded

Broken pieces can be strung together.
With bits of melted gold,
More often than not
They're bound by grit and soul

Sometimes I feel a little lost,
And often out of place,
I tell myself I'm meandering,
Taking it at my own pace,
Reinforcing the delusion that
I'm merely a spectator in this race

It's just a little out of sync,
Half-formed thoughts, memories hazed,
Waiting for the world to blink,
Peripheral vision blurry, demeanour unfazed.

It all makes sense in my mind,
The contexts and actions intertwined,
The words escape, twisting my clarity.
A hopeful gift, a fleeting reality

Throws off balance,
Disconnected even as I integrate,
Searching for absolution &
respect in retrograde,
But mostly, I long for a place to belong.
And it's quiet, calm bliss, where I feel sure and strong

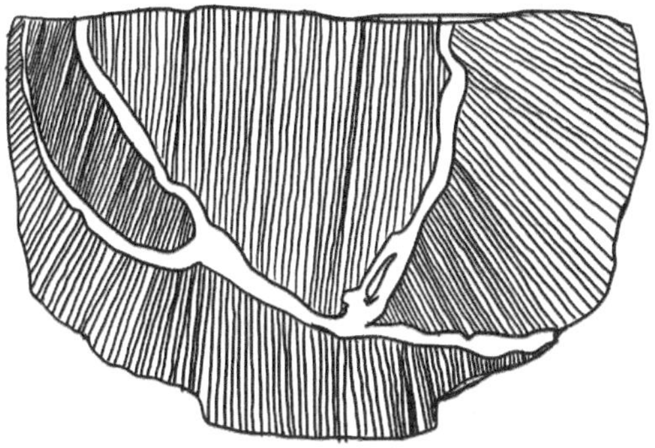

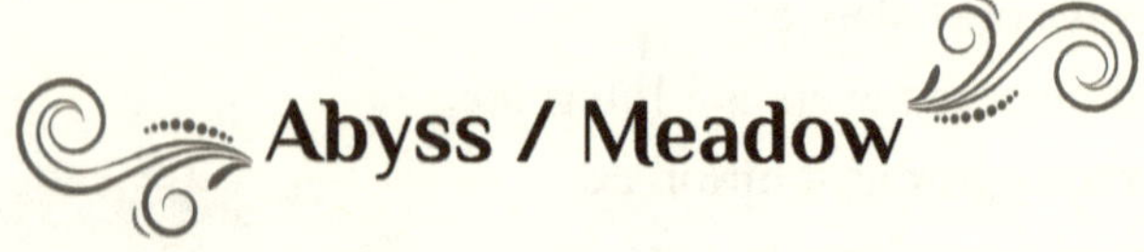

Abyss / Meadow

I looked out at the darkness,
While it stared right back at me,
Trying to decipher this lonely child
Shrouded in mystery

A cool whisper breathes through my hair,
A gentle caress,
A reminder that it'll always be there.

In that moment, I can't help myself –
Fists clenched,
Fire coursing through me,
I hurl a shout at the edge of the world,
And hear its echoes calling me,

I shout and scream and fight,
Until I finally breathe

As I stand there shuddering,
My eyes are ablaze – defiant
A single pearl gives me away.

Although everything remains silent
There I stay, trapped in myself,
Lost to sight and sound,
Of the beautiful meadow behind me,
Waiting for me to turn around

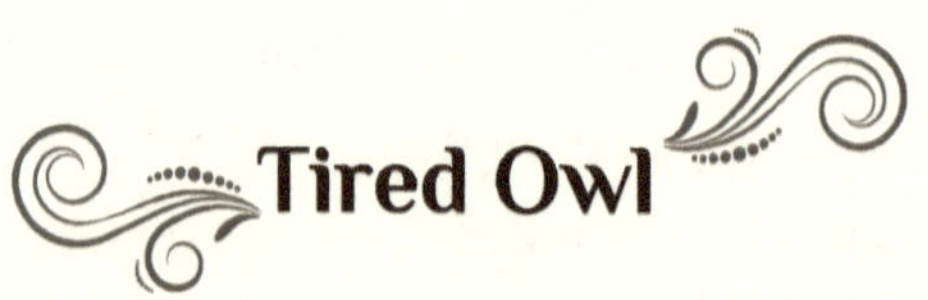

Tired Owl

Trapped somewhere deep in an enchanted wood,
A tired old owl on a lone log stood,
Watching as the night paled into day,
Watching as the seasons gently rolled away.
Afraid to blink,
Afraid of not letting a moment sink,
Ridding himself of every chance to think

He whispered his thoughts to the whispering trees,
Hoping the wind might set his soul free.
But time only listened, silent and vast,
A trickster who promised peace at last.

Time was his captor, his most trusted friend,
A circle unbroken: No start, no end
And he kept its steadfast company,
Cheated into believing he'd have a moment of peace in
the end.

Supernova – Musings of a Dying Star

I was beautiful once,
Lighting up the lives around me,
They gathered close, drawn to my warmth,
Basking in my glow, enjoying my company.

Something inside me was changing,
Maybe I was growing up, maybe it was time,
I didn't understand the darkness I felt,
Except to realise that it was mine.

They wanted more from me,
And so I bargained myself away,
Sold my soul to the rest of the universe,
To have company for just another day
To have something worth holding onto,
To somehow feel okay

And so I gave myself away,
I gave and I gave and I gave and I gave,
Until one day,
I broke.
I burned.
I caved.

All those around watched in horror and awe,
As my brilliance surrounded them,
Drawing everything into myself,
Leaving them blinded, hurting and raw

And yet, they marvelled at the magnificent sight,
Looking on calmly as I imploded with all my might,
A devastation meant for the ages,
My sorrow and anger broke through all my cages.

A supernova –
A breathtaking, violent piece of art.
Destroying everything in my path,
As I fell apart.

The silence that followed was strange.
The echoes and voices started to fade,
A world once bursting with life and sound
Now nothing, just empty space all around.

Yet, I wander, looking for my pieces,
Scattered across the universe as they are,
The powerful remnants of a painfully dying star

A mosaic of all that we love.
That's who we are
Broken pieces that fit together,
Searching and rebuilding, both near and far.

Until the person I see in front of me,
Is the person I know myself to feel,
Is the person I know myself to be.

Because I Know I Am (Low-Key Soliloquy)

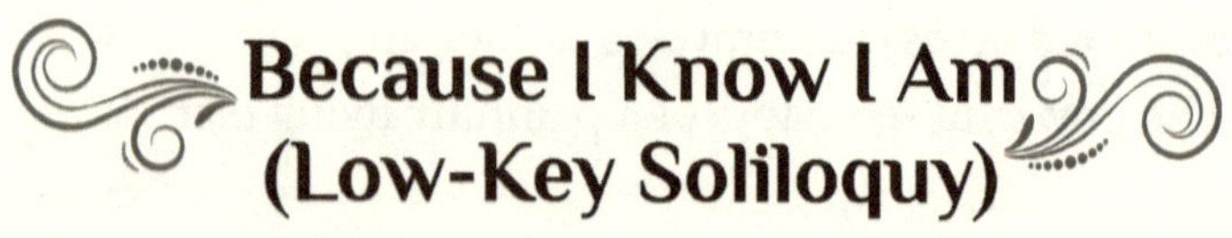

Do you ever feel like you're running away?
Leaving everything behind,
    Wind in your sails,
        Drenched in glowing hopes & borrowed
        sunshine.
Suitcases packed and repacked endlessly,
    Trips line up at every turn,
        Like you have nowhere to be,
        & just some money to burn
Caught in a devious dichotomy,
Because I know I am.

Do you ever feel like you're trying to stay?
Trying to find someplace that feels like home,
Somewhere safe,
    Surrounded, but alone.
Where everything feels comfortable, familiar, known,
    Where you can come and go as you please,
    Routine will keep things exactly the same, you
    see.
Stopped by the roots that you have grown,
Because I know I am.

Do you ever feel like you're falling apart?
Like everything chips away at another piece,
  You built those with your own hands,
  From everything you knew at that moment,
    In a way that you understand
Torn to shreds by some manic beast,
  & yet, it's you in the mirror,
  Trying to make room for something clearer
From your melted mess of mind, body & hand, you
search for relief.
Because I know I am.

Do you ever feel like you're trying to change?
  Holding on to what matters to you,
  Trying to make sense of what you think and do,
Marking out things you'd like to start anew,
Reaching for the standard set up for you,
  Hyperventilating, making the most of what
  you've got, heedlessly,
  Solving, resolving, rushing through the two
  steps you see in your path,
  Going after that ever-changing belief,
  relentlessly.
Tired, confused and deeply battered,
Because I know I am.

Do you ever feel like you're trying to be okay?
To somehow, magically, mystically, make
it through the day?
    The thoughts in your head don't find a way,
    They fester, build, and complicate,
To somehow not bring gloom and sadness with the
things you say,
    To somehow understand it all at once,
    As though it's certain and unmoving,
      & not weighing on your head a tonne
Heaving, living, loving, breathing.
Because I know I am.

 I Wanted To Be A Runaway

I always knew that someday,
I'd just sit in a car and drive away.

I had no love for whimsical goodbyes,
For promises wrapped in empty lies
Or the weight of hollow, saddened eyes

All my life I ran –
       Sometimes unintentionally,
But mostly by design, by plan

In solitude, I found my bliss.
cut off from every source of happiness
I escaped into my own abyss.

I'd return for a while, leave a mark,
then vanish, fading into the dark

Shrouded in my own suspense
To the world, I never made sense.
And nobody searched for the door through my battered
fence

Until a simple 'hi'
Which led to a who, a what, a how, and a why
Couldn't they see?
That I just wanted the world to leave me be?

Fortunately or unfortunately
(For that verdict, we shall wait)
I took the bait

With a leap of faith
I fell in love with something that I could not craft or
master,
I fell in love with the sound of laughter.

I no longer longed to disappear into the sunset glow,
I wanted it to be the backdrop to my story – my happy
ever after

Once a myth and now a fantasy
I found someone who would never let me be.

A grip to reality,
The first step towards my legacy
And as I look down at the rungs below
It's incredible that this began with a 'hello'.

I had dreamed of a great (albeit quiet) escape.
Now, I dream of playing the cello.
All thanks to some stubborn fellow.

I wanted to be a runaway,
But somehow,
You convinced me to stay.

RADIANT REFLECTIONS

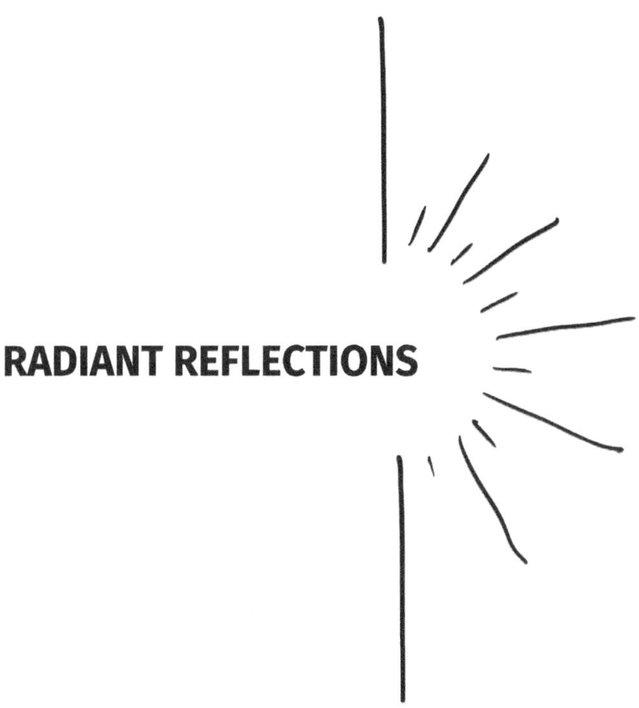

Puppies

They are beauty,
They are grace,
They will lick you in the face.

You walk towards them at the end of a harrowing day,
They don't really care what you want to do or say,
They just really, really want to play.

Small little beady eyes look at you from their home:
Tail wagging, safely tucked in their bed,
Hoping for a belly rub, a hello, or at least a pat on the
head.

Everything must be climbed and explored!
"I've played with this for 0.3 seconds, and now I'm bored."
Every footstep means a brand new friend!
"Okay, enough touching, this really must end."

"I'm off on an adventure,
To wherever, just you see!"
No, no, just stop following me!

I'll run around and dig,
I'll run around and lick,
I'll run in all the circles,
And I'll even play with a stick,
I'll eat all of it and fight for every little bite,
STOP CALLING ME CUTE, DON'T YOU SEE
ALL MY MIGHT

And now that's done, I can explore again some more,
From here, from there,
From every nook to every shore,
But first, I need a quick nap.
I'm tired to my entire core.

Trusting eyes nodding off to sleep,
Leaving you with just soft touches to keep,
A gentle pat,
Fingers running through the warm fur,
As their eyes droop shut,
Well, that's that!

Radio

The first click leads to a loud boom,
A sound that swallows up the room –
Someone grins and boldly takes a stance,
Demanding an impromptu dance

Laughter spills into every space,
Everyone lost in the rhythm's pace
Until the dials spin around,
Taking a chance on the next sound,

This time we're partly amused,
By the absolutely absurd ruse,
Some listeners may be enthused
Of calling up a stranger and pretending to be confused

A shout of protest somewhere in the back,
Snaps the tiny box back onto track,
A lilting melody, soft and warm.
Wraps you up in lovely charm
Eyes closed, swaying slowly,
Losing yourself in the song's gentle flow

Reality jars,
A radio jockey reads your upcoming stars,
Before there's a break of 27 hours,
Packed with ads for schemes, flats, and cars

It's strange how many voices you hear.
In the few moments you tune in for the traffic report,
Stories told far and near
Waiting for the host to confirm your fear

Suddenly, an old favourite plays
Transporting you to another time, another place,
You sing it loud, off-key but free,
Proud: the lyrics are etched in memory.

The last note fades, and you sigh,
A song, a moment, a fleeting high.
Somehow, this small act made you feel,
Younger, refreshed and quite content,

And so finally, you relent.
Letting that old little device rest,
Until the time you tune in next,
Wondering what surprise it'll manifest!

# Clouds

I close my eyes as I try to fall asleep,
But they're open wide: your gaze cuts deep,

The sun breaks through: Its golden hue
Reflected in drops of the morning dew,
With endless blue skies unfolding around you.

You are everything, yet nothing at all,
Drifting giants, waiting for imagination's call,
Becoming a castle, a dragon, a ship set to sail,
That whisper of mist tells a wandering tale.

You shape the sky, with tales untold,
Bringing wonder and bold stories
Bringing shame to the persistent old lady on the moon,
Your fleeting beauty: here for a moment, and gone too
soon.

I watch you floating by,
Hugging the curves of the endless sky.
I see you thundering far away,
The lightning courses through your veins,
Getting me to hide from you,
But I can't help but stay,

Because I'm mesmerised by your spectacle,
Your spirit, your charm,
Beautiful and delectable.

You glide past me, fading into the blue –
New shapes forming in the morning's soft hue
But the tears of your breaking form,
Fall as raindrops, gentle and warm.
Your brilliant journey slowly erased.
In your quiet grace, a soft endless space.

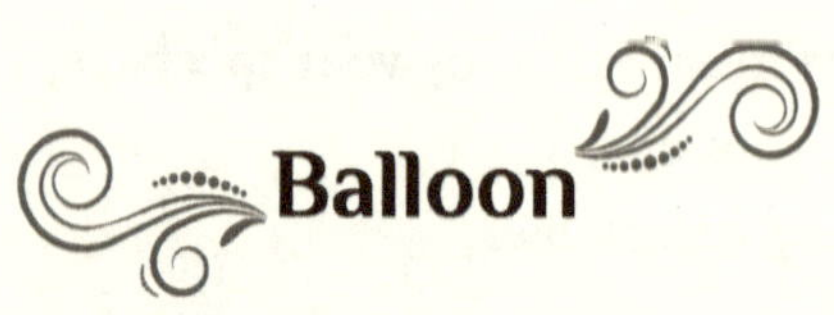

Balloon

"And sometimes I think, we are all balloons with long strings" – Leigh Neuage

I set out on an adventure today:
Although it sounds quite strange to say,
The strings at my feet, they tugged away,
But for once, I was determined to go astray.

I wandered, I'd floated through the streets of old,
Listening to all the stories they told,
Tales of the time when I was small,
When I felt invincible, ready for it all.

Heading back to the things I loved the most,
I paused for a chat with a friendly ghost
I bounced from place to place,
Smiles reflecting on my happy face

The spring in my step never left that day,
As I took several deep breaths and let the wind carry me away,
Down the streets that scared me back then,
Running through my favourite hideouts again

When I paused for a breath, I tried something new,
I read a book, painted, sang, danced, played,
Just everything that I thought was long overdue.
I think I was nearly at my happiest then,
Tired, optimistic, and somehow also content

And then the gentle tug at my feet reminded me,
Of the things calling for me

But today's adventure filled me with an odd spirit,
It took me back to my childhood, if only just for a
minute,
Simpler times, that's for sure,
But I am who I am because of what I endure.

Today's adventure gave me the strength to get back and
do,
Everything and anything that I wanted to

"I have something right now and it's all that I've got"
What I have is today, and it's really a lot"

DESIRES & DREAMS

Entangled

In the hours when twilight faded into day
In a place not far away
They sat,
In Silence – their comforting friend
Paused with bated breath,
Each waiting to hear what the other said.

With a crooked smile, a hushed whisper –
He moved the conversation forward.
She laughed
For an instant, his world echoed the sound
That beautiful symbol of life, pure & profound.

The corridor was deserted.
Just them – imagination, stories & fandom
With chins in their hands,
Lying outside the battered door,
Their gazes locked –
They needed nothing more.

He played her favourite tune
And they danced in the light of the moon.
Not together – just having fun –
In the moment with that special someone.

Singing – like nobody could hear
Disturbing sleeping creatures that thrived near
They sat with everything entangled.
Beneath the sky that was star-spangled

No want, no need, no reason why.
Just them and the dark sky
And the twinkle in their eye

For that night, they remained,
Together as they were –
Original, unexplained;
Purely human,
Effortlessly in sync,
Imperfectly understood
Before the sun comes
Bringing with it things good.

Intertwined – souls mingling
Steady breaths, senses tingling.

In that night,
They were infinite

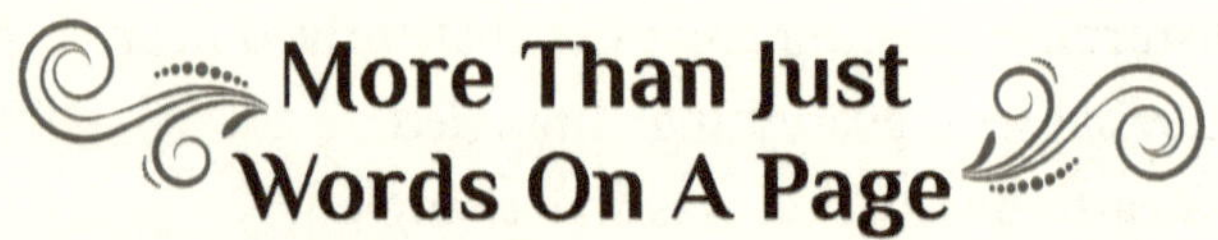

More Than Just Words On A Page

That night, they were more than just words on a page
They were the players of the stage.

Snowflakes landing gently on their noses,
Watching dewdrops on the blooming roses
Caffeine addicts brewed their early morning doses:
Chilly winds whispering as the world reposes

They danced like ballerinas, on their twinkle toes,
They ran through streets and knocked on doors
Searching upright or on all fours
Lost & bewildered in the world of prose

Like nightingales chiming across the sky
With smiles – beautiful, forced, or wry
The tides were low, the tides were high.
Some are bold, & some shy.

Bright & twinkling stars were they.
Crackled & burnt, didn't fade away
Painting the fortunes of the coming day,
With the leftovers from yesterday

They achieved their every dream.
In shades of brown, violet, gold & cream
Liberated, yet bound:
In the fairy tales & fantasies, they were found.

Across bridges & palaces of ice
With glowing stones, dragons & mice
And so, the river flows along its bed,
With frogs & logs & the occasional detached head

Through the castle halls, they roamed
Fireplaces, machines, creaked and groaned.
Ties, courtesies, giggles & films
What would they rather have today?
Tails, hooves, wings or gills?

Through every trial, triumph, and fall,
The observers watched and criticised it all.
And yet, they looked on,
Enthralled.

Stumbling, pouncing, prancing along
At the end, they stood tall & strong.
To prove some right
And to prove most wrong

Myriad

Cloaked in wisdom, covered in shame
Your tongue still reaching for their name,
Somehow, their boats stayed afloat
The dark, alluring, dusty moat

Sharp blades, sharper words
They each got what they deserved.
Hand in hand, they danced to their song
Together, they belong.

They conquered the world at large,
The parts, the hills, the ancient barge.
With a whisper, & a slight twist
Sparkling, twinkling,
Intertwined with the mist

They faded away, no longer crystal clear
Leaving behind something to hold dear.
Every step became history,
They transformed into a mystery

That night, they were more than words on the page.
The heroes, the damsels, the artists, the sage,
Writers of stories, creators of letters,
Never overshadowed by their betters

They were more than just words on a page
That night, they were the life of their stage.

Penny Jar

He traded his nights beneath the stars
For an empty heart
And a full penny jar

A jar full of promise
A jar full of happiness
A jar full of potential bliss

Through the bustling streets,
He'd freely roam,
Far from the alleyway
He once called home

At first, the clinking pennies in his pocket,
Made him feel like he could buy a rocket,
Tucked under his arm, the jar gave him courage and
strength
For he was no longer shunned wherever he went.
But he wasn't... content?
That was a word he'd heard
From one who seemed quite absurd
He wasn't sure what she meant...

And so, he decided to use the pennies for a task,
He'd create the most perfect mask
And be for once who he wanted to be.
And with his pennies, he'd shape his reality.

He changed his voice and his clothes.
His insecurity and his pose,
(And gained some height by standing on his toes)

He used the half-filled jar.
For things that seemed, to him, bizarre.
He used them for songs
He used them to correct several wrongs
He used them to watch his favourite dance.
And jousts with the glorious lance.
With ladies and lords, he stayed,
And suffocated the tiny part of him that felt betrayed.

His jar became emptier,
And his heart remained the same,
But he was the only one to blame.

At last,
There came a day when just one penny remained,
With gifts and rewards,
His dependence on his jar had changed drastically.

But that single penny.
How it clanged and how it clattered
As though its presence were all that mattered
He stared at it for over an hour.
"It was quiet when it had a few more for company."
His mood was sour
And he wished that this penny.
Would let him be

All his life he'd traded in pennies,
And nothing made him feel richer than these.

And now only one remained.
One symbol to remind him
Of how everything had changed.
But he had to put his armour on,
He was weak
But he had to stay strong.
Otherwise, they would break him,
And he'd rather keep his story long.

He became a breaker instead,
Shattering glass, a rush of dread
As he walked away, feverish and red
Along with the jar,

It felt as though he had shattered his soul.
But as the last penny rolled away,
He felt strangely

Whole?

SERENADES & STORIES

Princess

& so she twirled from arm to arm.
Allured by their charm,
The brave knights watched
The kingdom's future shift from hand to hand
They see it clearly from where they stand.

A thousand days ago, the fight had begun
One that brought out the warrior in every son.
Songs written
Maidens smitten
& the battlefields with their blood
Were soon wiped out by harvests and floods.

The valiant King,
With his bright emerald ring,
Watched from the Dais
Watched them all,
Watched that fateful ball,
Without love or bias.

For tonight, the princess would make her choice.
And with her engagement, the whole kingdom would
rejoice.

The King was troubled, you see,
And his feisty daughter refused to bend the knee.
"It's for your own good."

Fourteen hours later,
She agreed,
Claiming that she finally understood
& she saw now the path that would take her,
From maiden,
To her complete womanhood.

& so she danced with her suitors through the night
But none of them seemed 'just right'.

Until.
One knight, dressed in white,

Rugged, scarred, handsome

His appearance filled the onlookers with fright.

& to this soul, she was drawn.

This was one

She wouldn't mind waiting from dusk to dawn
Or perhaps bear his spawn?

The knight presented her with a rose.
She pricked herself on its thorns
As he pulled her close

She gasped as the blood flowed along her arm.

She seemed to be in a trance.

As he clutched her hand tighter and continued to dance

Never once wavering in his act of charm.

She looked him in the eye,
& saw what she should have seen from the start

He was an Angel,
With a Demon's heart.

She returned to her chambers that night.
Confused and frustrated

Everybody insisted he was kind, just might
Be the perfect 'other half' for her

Oh, that gorgeous knight!

Seething, she looked at the faint scars on her wrist.
She vowed to always remember this.

Later, the bells were rung.
& many joyous songs were sung,

For both the 'lovers' were dressed in white.
The beautiful princess & her brave knight.

As time passed,
Although their marriage seemed to last,
The princess always glimpsed his cruelty,
& when she erred, she paid her penalty,
For the thorns were replaced with other things.
And though he gave her riches and rings
and conquered a hundred kings,

Her heart, for him, was never warm.

As she struggled to remain
In the eye of his storm.
The only one aware of his reality was she.
To the rest of the world,
'Perfect' was all he seemed to be,

She waited,
& instead told tales of her love
Her beloved; her sweet, innocent dove.

Yet, something had changed,

For the knight had been feeling quite strange.
He wanted to be better
(But he was the best!)

He wanted to be with her.
(Imagining her laugh... what was that feeling in his chest?)

He wanted to be gentle.

He wanted to be kind.

For her.

For she was always on his mind.

He wanted to see her smile,
Wanted to make her heart beat faster
As though she had just run a mile.
But alas!

The knight knew nothing but cruelty.
It was his way of showing her he cared, you see?
(Quite twisted, isn't he?)

One day, he realised he was in love,
With his sweet, innocent, perfect little dove

& he swore that he would show her how much she
meant to him,
How she filled him with rainbows & sunshine, quite
up to the brim.

& so he bought a bouquet of roses.
and headed home to tell her the truth
He would wait for his affection to bear fruit.

He entered

"I'm home!" he called.

& in an instant, he was mauled.

By his own spear

At the blunt end stood his beloved dear,

As their eyes met,

For once, she laughed as he wept.

As he crumpled to the ground,
She whispered her words, profound.

"They thought you were the perfect half of my broken,
battered soul,

But what they did not see,
Was that I was already whole.

I am the woman I was supposed to be.

I choose to be complete, like I chose my gown,

I choose to be the one who wears a crown."
It is said that she was the best Queen

Her reign was longer and more prosperous than anyone
had seen,

She reminded everyone,

That although she was gentle and wore a dress,

She was always more, never less,

For there was none as brave, beautiful, or valiant

As a Princess.

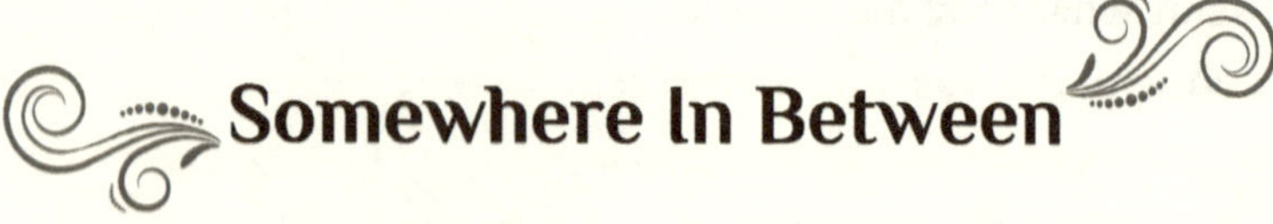 Somewhere In Between

In the stage of life we're at
        It often seems,
                Like we're stuck,
                        Somewhere in between

Somewhere between who you are and who you want
to be,
Being yourself,
        Yet changing constantly

Somewhere between those times in life
        Where everyone knows exactly what to do,
Except of course,
        The ones doing a group project with you

Somewhere between those existential crises when
everything's falling apart,
        Convincing yourself that it is fine,
Taking the chaos day by day,
        One questionable life decision at a time

Somewhere between chasing vibrant hopes & dreams,
& watching rapidly falling self-esteem,
Wondering if you'll ever get this right

Maybe tomorrow? This week? This year?
Tonight?

Somewhere between being a functioning human being,
& knowing that eating straight out of the pan
Means one less bowl to clean.

Somewhere between one step forward and two steps
back,
Like exploring a new domain,
        Just to discover how many more skills you lack

Somewhere between taking the road less travelled,
Even though you know it's tough and will probably
make you cry,
Wondering if it's wiser to accept,
To quit, to settle, or just to get by.

Somewhere between not knowing how you got through
the day because you had absolutely no more energy,
& still saying "yes" to spontaneous plans, as tiring and
chaotic as they may be

Somewhere between living life your way,
        Distilling every moment of it,
& shutting it all out,
        Focusing on getting through today

Somewhere between wanting to see the world,
& not wanting to leave bed,
          You just settle for a nice, long walk instead.

Somewhere between wanting pauses at work too,
& then not knowing what else to do

Somewhere between knowing that there are no right
answers anymore,
& hoping for some clarity,
Just to feel confident & secure

Somewhere between indulging in retail therapy,
& realising – there's no more space, so now where will
you keep these?

Somewhere between knowing the support and
encouragement you're getting from those you call your
own,
Knowing, on some level, that some roads must be
walked alone

Somewhere between the future and the past,
Suspended in purgatory where everything feels
permanent,
Yet nothing is built to last.

Somewhere between eating healthily
     & eating your feelings – just as cake,
Somewhere between elaborate meals,
     & anything that takes under 15 minutes to
make

Somewhere between wanting to stand up for what you
believe,
& pausing – learning from what you perceive

Somewhere between wanting to be in effortless glam,
     & being too tired to actually give a damn

Somewhere between wide-eyed and open heart,
& gradually opening up your inner fortress,
     Cautiously lowering your guard –
     Not much progress, but it's a start.

Some days feeling amazing, like an absolutely
wonderful, powerful queen,
& some days feeling like nothing at all,
     Stuck somewhere in between

Somewhere between home and away,
Rooted in what you know,
Adapting to where you stay,
     Living with a jet-lagged heart,
     Believing that it'll all be okay

Somewhere between tomorrow and today
        Not entirely sure where we're going,
                Or how to get there,
but,
        At least
        We're on our way

Stained Glass Windows

Stained glass windows make the world look so strange,
The same world,
      Distorted and coloured,
           By a frantic, wavering gaze

It seems like just a trick of light,
      Making it appear so differently,
           It's hard to shake off the feeling,
                That there's truth in what you see

I wonder what it's like to live in a stained glass window,
Would you believe everyone's descriptions?
Or trust in what you know?
Would you wrestle through occlusion, reflection and
every tiny crack?
Or simply accept what instinctively seems like a fact?

Maybe you'd present declarations,
      "The sky is blue," you'd scream.
While the others around you would shake their heads
in dismay,
Insisting that it was rather a lovely shade of cream

Maybe you'd accept it as hallucinations –
For who needs sense to find peace,
For the rest, it could be unbridled imaginations,
A fish casually climbing up a tree

At some point, exasperation would set in –
     A natural outcome of conflicting views,
        Compromise, they say, is where change
        begins,
Treating another's truth as an alternate universe is news.

What a strange world it would be,
     If each of us looked through our own stained
     glass,
     What if we traded them for a moment?
     Instant insanity? Or reveal something similar,
     but new?

Perhaps, over time, we'd carry a unique tinge of
desperation,
Our own cracks, chips, and dust,
     The subtle scars of attempted navigation

Perhaps that's how we find each other,
From deep within the walls of fractured glass walls
When the glimmers and shadows achieve a feat,
Of momentary understanding,
      Colours interweaving,
          A momentary visual treat,
A reminder that, crazy though I may be,
      Crazy though it would seem,
      For a moment, I am not alone.

Creativity

A brushstroke on a canvas,
    With love and a sigh,
    The merging colours,
       The shaded sky,
    A moment captured,
       Any onlooker, enraptured

What is creativity?
    It is the art of letting people see

The resonating beats,
    The clapping hands,
       The thumping feet,
That one awkward jiggle,
    The one touch that left a tingle,
    Closing your eyes, letting it wash over you.

What is creativity?
    It is the art of making people feel

Soft hums of the well-known song,
    A lullaby, or an earworm,
    Just taking you along

The notes that fly through your throat, mind, and hands,
The ones that make you feel like someone understands,
Your thoughts are engulfed by the harmony
        As it flows from your head to your feet

What is creativity?
        It is the art of letting people breathe.

Bold, firm words,
        Clear meaning & direction,
Passion-driven sentences that make you stand up and say,
        That you want to make a change today.
Emboldened, enlightened, and promising,
        and always willing to listen to anyone about
        anything

What is creativity?
        It is the art of making people believe

In the corner, through it all,
They sit taking notes,
Recording achievements and inside jokes
        Armed with their eyes, their wit, and a pen,
        They chronicle the antics of all men,

Not disturbing or depriving
        Just hopeful, just striving

What is creativity?
It is the art of letting people be.

Wanderings in Time

Have you ever noticed that tales often begin
With a simple "Once Upon a Time"?

Time & stories,
Both fleeting forms of meaning,
Seem so tangible, but are deceiving,
Moving through simple, fantastic experiences,
All facts gliding smoothly in a line –

For the truth in every novel, rhyme or scene,
Is that it starts somewhere,
& ends somewhere else,
Merely describing a transcendent in between

An exercise in futility, it would seem,
No rational purpose,
Just a captured thought or dream
Floating aimlessly in a world, otherwise bleak,

And yet, adding colour and creativity
With a tone of endless possibility,
Granting courage to those bold enough to seek,
And lending strength to those who feel weak

Capturing the wanderings of an idle mind,
But more often, escapades when the stars align,
And in those words,
Deftly cementing an existence in time.

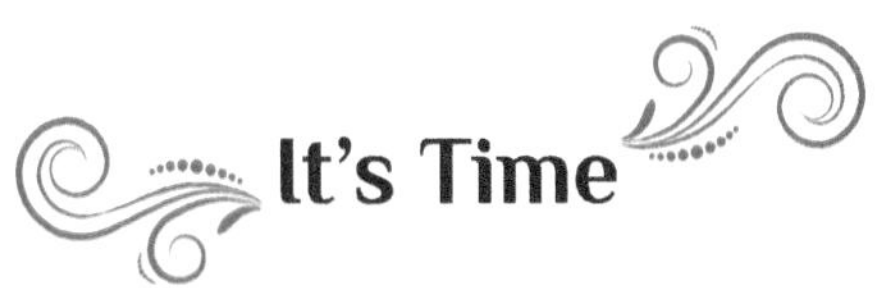

It's Time

There's a picture of us I often see,
Etched in my mind like a fading memory,
It's almost as if you are standing right next to me.

Everything feels hazy, a bit obscure,
But that fits – it's never happened before,
This story unfolds with trolleys in tow.
Right through the gates of Terminal 4

In the waiting room, an unexpected delay,
We wanted to leave but had to stay,
As people passed, we lingered on.
Waiting together, in solace and strength,
Even though we were tired, we spent

You wouldn't see us broken if you looked at us,
You wouldn't see it, even if you tried,
Not in our faces, nor in our stride
Because we laughed through whatever life threw at us,
As much as everything inside us cried

That's how I'll remember it:
Going through things, pretending we had a clue,

And then laughing about the ridiculous messes we got
ourselves into.

We could have gone through it all alone, you see,
And managed just fine, given our skill and capability,
But everything felt lighter, easier and freer
Simply because of the company

Then the first flight was set to start,
One by one, we would all depart,
It seemed surreal in that part

This is what we'd been waiting for.
Then why was it so bittersweet?
Why was that moment unsure?

I watched our roads begin to part,
As you stepped forward on your chosen path
I held on tighter, afraid to let go –
For everything I had been, everything I know,
And everyone who held a piece of my heart

At last, it was my turn to go,
I stepped forward –
Excited, terrified, and alone
I stepped forward,

And that was that
I stepped forward,
And never looked back.

For a while, I pressed ahead, unshaken, headstrong,
Carrying my uncertainty and loneliness along,
Until one day, I missed you,
Out of habit, I turned to my side –
And found, to my surprise,
You were there
Just a little further away,
You called me an idiot and went on to say,
That you'd been waiting for me to look your way

That's when I realised – they were all around,
Some waltzing by, some trudging the ground,
Some moving loudly, and some without a sound

And so,
I walked on,
A lot more courage and faith in my stride.

Because deep down,
I knew

It was time.

For you to live your life,
and for me to live mine.

EPILOGUE

Story Time

In my stories, you'll find me in my purest form,
Existing vibrantly outside of expectations and the norm,
Free from the exhausting complexities of reality,
A safe haven, where I can just be

It wouldn't be a permanent solution, of course,
I enjoy the hustle just as much as the pause.

I live inside these princesses,
Twirling their way through the starlit skies,
Not waiting to be rescued,
Chasing dreams with fearless eyes,
& inside them warriors with daggers drawn,
Fighting battles until dawn

I live inside my stories, you see,
In them, you'll find the scattered pieces of me.

The heart of a warrior,
Courage of a clan,
Worlds I spin & unravel,
The fleeting whims of a scribbling hand

In my stories, you will find me,
Cast in words of drama & make-believe

Quietly lurking in the shadows,
With the mysterious air of secrets untold,
Setting the scene & putting all the parts in place,
Before taking up my role centre stage,
Describing the battle, the thrill, the chase,
Anything to make you turn the page.

Riveted as I am to tales of old,
Adding each adventure to my personal lore,
Figuring out the elements, the twists, the flow,
Embellishing or just making things up as I go,
Ensuring I do justice to the story that's being told,
Intertwining the pieces, with bits of my soul

There are words, fantasies, & stories inside my head.
They'll be gone like me one day – forgotten, dead,
But hopefully not if I write them out instead.

Maybe that's why I get to know people by their story,
Not in that list of places they were or plan to be,
But the things that changed them,
        Touched them,
        Scarred them.
        For better or for worse,

Raw emotional humanity,
A beautiful curse,

Those stories fall out almost as though they're well-
rehearsed,
Spun around in our own minds
Cleaned & polished, now resembling a verse,
Whispered to one another in the middle of the night,
Whispered & laced with intent, impact & might,
Whispered in those quiet moments of peace,
When the mood feels just right

& maybe that's why,
If you ask me nicely,
I might just tell you a story tonight.

YOU'RE ALL MIME

A narrative play

You're All Mime

And so, it began.
It wasn't much, just a glimpse on the streets,
It wasn't much, just a gentle breeze,
It wasn't much, just a heart skipping a beat.
How it began, he would never know,
How it ended is the story of this show.
He started as a normal man.
A human man.

Armed with a stubborn, irrational, determined will; and some limited acting skill, James William was he. The first, the best, the only, you see.

His partner in crime and only friend was William Holmes. Misfits to the very end. In their first few years at a public school, they'd made paper planes together, to look cool. The students loved them, the teachers did not. In fact, one gave them a jar and told them to fill it with stamp-paper planes within the hour. William was doubtful, James was not. He began and never stopped. At the end of the hour, the jar was full. The count stood at forty-two thousand, seven hundred and two. Of course, they were kicked out by the teacher's shiny white shoe. Not just them, their jar too.

The two were inseparable, more with than without. They'd sing, play, and usually prance about. Their favourite song was one they sang to each other every day. It was the one thing that could never lead them astray. And so, they'd sing to each other all the while: "My Bonnie lies over the ocean, my Bonnie lies over the sea". They'd sing to make the world seem normal, and then they'd sing to make each other smile.

Until the one fateful day, that William got on a flight that didn't make it through the night. His paper airplane was burnt, they say, but James has it in his pocket unto this very day. They left each other in reality but stayed together in James' mind. Because no matter what he lost, William he could always find. They laughed and talked and sang, just as they always had. To James, it was perfect, although everyone else seemed sad. He tried to show them, but they never saw his friend. They told him that he should just forget James because William had met his end.

James tried to believe them, but he just never could. He spoke to William more than they said he should. But he found comfort in the company he had chosen. Their friendship remained as strong as it was, preserved and frozen. Everything was well.

But a strange black cloud strayed over them that day. During recess, they all went out to play. The playground bullies decided that James was their target today. They taunted him and called him names, until William stood and nearly stamped on everybody else's games. (Tiny people they were, and tiny games)

He screamed and yelled.

And those bullies laughed it off.

They called him names, mocked his tiny hands and tiny games, and then left.

That night, they returned.

They beat him up in an alley on his way home. They plucked out a fingernail, twisted his hair, 'Scream,' they said, 'No one can hear you. And no one will come even if they do. Nobody has or ever will love you.'

He was younger than them by nearly ten years, and yet they used their entire strength until he was broken, battered, and in tears.

William found him there. He sang their song. James and William, through sticks and stones. Together through broken windows and broken bones.

But James.

Well.

That was the day he lost his trust;
In magic and pixie dust.

And he decided that if the world was this way,
To it, or to them, he had nothing more to say.

And since that day,
He never spoke.

His actions did.
Louder than the words of most.
He was everyone's source of happiness, ever the gracious host.
But his voice was gone,
Like the mist of a ghost.

And they both grew, James William and William Holmes. Both in their heads and in their bones.

Fast forward to today's wintry day.

The town was peaceful; there was a chill in the air. Cuddled in their warm jackets and simple cloaks, they drifted between lampposts.

On the middle of the street stood James in his prime.

The great, the glorious, the spectacular, the mime!

He did everything they expected him to do.

Trapped himself in a box, sunk to the ground,

Offered flowers to a few,

Was pulled away by an invisible string,

He mimed his way through everything.

Until he heard a quiet voice sing

"My Bonnie lies over the ocean,
My Bonnie lies over the sea,
My Bonnie lies over the ocean,
Oh, bring back my Bonnie to me."

He paused

The crowd was confused.

But his legs and hands refused to move.

Far away in the distance, a beauty he had seen

One who shone with all the world's sheen

She was singing their song!

And her lilting voice reached his aching ears,

And left them ringing.

He snapped himself out of it and continued his act.

Be realistic, he told himself, deal with the facts.

When his work was done and the money poured in, the people moved on about their lives, and he followed his tempting sin.

He watched her from afar.

She sat at a coffee table with a friend. Her eyes seemed unfocused, as though she had never belonged in the living world; but surely she was far too beautiful to be dead?

He watched for a while longer.

And as he watched, the feelings inside him seemed to grow stronger.

He felt whole and complete,

Like he could build a house, right there in the middle of the street.

He felt a surge of happiness, and everything seemed like it was made of all things good,

With some care, and maybe the glimpse of eternal bliss,

He looked at her, sure that she was worth it,

For everything that he had seen, he knew he could face,

The good, the bad, the ugly, all of it, with grace,

As long as she was with him,

And he was with her,

Her thoughts, her dreams,

With her smile, her laughter.

And so, he began dreaming of their happily ever after.

She was plain and simple,

She even had a tiny dimple.

She spoke with gestures and words,

She seemed knowledgeable, or so he had heard.

(From the voice inside his head, which isn't really absurd)

Through doves and white,

He watched her through the window, wishing for a glance with all his might,

She walked towards the door,

He tried to catch her eye,

She'd feel this too,

This rising pulse, this urge to pry,

Although she did seem distracted,

She had a smile on her face,

But she seemed exhausted and battered,

By what? He wasn't really sure. But he was an actor, and so he understood that the emotion mattered.

He wanted to say something, but words he never had.

And so, he decided to leave her be,

Even though the very prospect made him sad.

He kept a memory of her, created an image designed to stay,

Then he slowly, aimlessly walked away.

The song echoed in his head and in his ears. He thought back to her perfection, and just the thought left him in tears. He decided not to say anything to William just yet. He couldn't bear to share his basic story of regret. But as he sang his song in his mind that night, he sang it with just a little more conviction, making sure that the rhythm was just right. He sang it as he performed for his people through the streets and as he walked through the roads, walking from street to street.

But the world seemed to believe that things had to change,

Just when he thought he could go back to his normal life, something came back, something that brought back memories and rage,

As he walked through the streets, performing his art,

He suddenly spotted a face in the crowd,

A face that haunted his dreams and brought him back to the start,

And as the bully from his past laughed at him,

It was all he could do to keep his tears at a brim,

He stopped his sequence halfway and left,

He was just lucky that his collection was not a victim of theft,

But now the bully's face didn't seem to go away,

He'd worked so hard on looking at everything with an open view,

But the bully had seen him, that much he knew.

Recognised him too, maybe,

And if he did, now what?

What was he to do?

Run away like he did so many years ago?

Or just go on performing his show?

He felt broken that night,

And for several days, he couldn't look at his audience.

Without nearly shivering with fright.

When his angel had just begun to slip his mind, the world somehow left a sign for him to find. As he performed as usual on a regular day, the voice returned. And as it sang that beautiful song again, he found that his thoughts were on fire, but his mouth seemed to burn. He wanted to sing with her too. He wanted to find his Cinderella and give back her shoe. But he couldn't figure out what to do. She was leaving again, you see. And in that moment, he had a rush of adrenaline and shot off on a spree.

He stood in front of her and began a performance. As he went on, her friend would explain why they had stopped. And he watched her as her head dropped. She'd listen and quietly laugh. And he'd do something new, like splitting a potato in half.

Soon enough, it was all done, and it was time to go. Her friend gave him a few coins and thanked him for his show. The question remained on his tongue as she left him. How she knew his song, he'd never know. But he took it to mean that they were meant to be as one. Living out their days underneath the sun.

As she left, he slowly walked away.

Behind her, of course, but now, his thoughts were astray.

How would he confess?

How would he tell her how much he loved her?

How could he signal to her when she looked beautiful in her mother's dress?

With what would he impress her? The only thing he could do was mime, and she would never even see him. Why was he wasting his time?

He followed her nearly to the entrance of her home. He saw where she lived, turned into the nearest alley, and roamed. His feet took him to his favourite place.

His assigned meeting place with William, his saving grace.

William was at the park, waiting.

The two used their secret handshake before James collapsed on the nearby bench because he absolutely desperately needed a break.

William watched, concerned.

"What's wrong?" he asked, as James's insides churned.

He explained as much as he could, with his hands, eyes, sticks, and stones.

But this time, they weren't sufficient to explain the feeling that spread through his bones.

William seemed to understand.

He smirked and stood, offering James a hand.

"Maybe it's time you speak to this girl."

James nearly hit him.

For so many years, he'd kept his word,

Changing that for a chance with this girl!

Absurd!

And yet, he couldn't remove the thought from consideration.

After all, was it worth all the time it would take him? Was it worth the feeling of desperation?

Just a few words were all it would take,

And he was sure he could do that, for her sake,

Somehow, the thought just wouldn't leave him be,

Oh, how perfect she was!

When he opened his eyes again, William seemed scared.

He hesitated.

Upon a gesture from James, he elaborated.

"Maybe it's time for you to use your voice. I know you don't want to, but it's your choice."

James was amused but not too puzzled,

They'd been friends for so long,

Of course, William knew what was going on in his head.

The thought scared him too.

But he ignored the doubt and simply nodded instead.

William seemed surprised.

But he just nodded, and they continued to gesture and plan.

It was the perfect way to sweep this strange girl off her feet.

For now, her voice was playing in his head on repeat.

Armed with chocolates and clean clothes,

And a cliché necklace shaped like a heart,

James left William's company.

Shivering

He was dreading this part.

He walked to the gate that seemed familiar.

Already, he could hear her voice.

Would he really make this choice?

He stepped in,

Half, not completely yet

He wanted to take in the view.

And it was a precautionary measure against a ferocious pet.

He saw her sitting on a swing.

She looked beautiful, and he just wanted to wait for her to sing,

But just before he walked in,

She stood for a second or two,

Before calling out for a friend,

Who brought her a stick, and carefully placed near her, her shoes,

He watched as she fumbled and felt her way through it all,

Watched her as his soul shrank,

Making him feel small,

He wanted to leave; this couldn't be right.

It was a while before he accepted that she was gifted in everything but sight.

He was stunned, enraged, shattered,

And now, only his words mattered,

But could he say it after all?

How would they get by?

Would she accept him at all?

Through all the consideration, she began to sing,

And as she sang, the other memories returned,

From that old forgotten spring.

He remembered the face of the bully, the voice of his friend,

He remembered the time, the place,

He remembered his vow,

And everything that he was about to disgrace.

As he stood there, still, all he wanted to do was run,

How did everything end even before it had begun?

It didn't matter now.

Not a little.

Not at all.

He would have to leave this hope, this phantom hall.

Her friend left the swing and stepped into the house, perhaps to work on some little thing.

And suddenly, James's courage returned.

He should confess.

It was the first time he'd felt this way, and he must share with her what he had learned.

Not with words, that much he knew,

But his gesture could be a clue.

So he walked towards the swaying swing,

And placed his metallic necklace heart on her lap

Before wishing her a good day by tipping his cap.

She picked up the object, felt it, looking confused,

"Why are you giving me this?" she asked, amused.

Which is when he realised, again, that she couldn't see.

(That's the kind of idiot he was, wasn't he?)

He sighed, knelt,

And gestured his words to her.

She reached out, searching,

And touched him

He held her hand for a moment,

Before standing up

Suddenly, his energy seemed to be spent.

He walked away from the gate,

Got away from there before it was too late.

Courage, stubbornness and determination he had,

Words were what he seemed to lack.

He put his hands in his pockets and kept walking,

He never looked back.